THE LOST LAMB'S JOURNEY

5 Bedtime Stories of the Parables of Jesus

BLUME POTTER

INTRODUCTION

As you tuck your little ones into bed each night, you long for stories that not only captivate their imaginations but also nurture their hearts. The Lost Lamb's Journey: 5 Bedtime Stories of the Parables of Jesus is more than just a collection of bedtime tales—it's a gentle way to introduce your children or grandchildren to the timeless lessons of faith, love, and trust in God.

This book weaves together five beautifully illustrated stories based on the parables of Jesus, told through the eyes of the animals featured in these powerful teachings. Each chapter invites young readers into a world where they can learn about God's unending love, the importance of wise choices, and the potential for greatness within us all.

As you read these stories together, you'll not only be sharing meaningful moments of connection but also planting seeds of faith that can grow and flourish throughout your child's life. Whether it's the lost sheep, the birds of the air, or the mustard seed, each story is crafted to be both engaging and comforting, offering valuable life lessons that resonate with both young and old.

Let The Lost Lamb's Journey be a cherished part of your bedtime routine, creating memories and conversations that will last a lifetime. It's a must-have for any family seeking to bring the teachings of Jesus into the hearts of their little ones, one bedtime story at a time.

CHAPTER ONE:
THE LOST SHEEP

In a peaceful valley, surrounded by soft green hills, there lived a little lamb named Woolly. Woolly was a curious and playful lamb who loved to explore the meadow, nibbling on sweet grass and chasing butterflies. Every day, he followed the shepherd with the rest of the flock, feeling safe and content as long as he could see the other sheep around him.

But one day, Woolly's curiosity got the best of him. As he wandered a bit too far, he found a patch of clover that looked especially tasty. He nibbled and nibbled, not realizing that he was drifting away from the flock. When he finally looked up, the hills were silent, and the familiar sounds of the other sheep had faded away. Woolly was alone.

Panic set in as Woolly realized he was lost. The sky began to darken, and the valley that once felt so safe now seemed big and scary. He bleated loudly, hoping the other sheep or the shepherd would hear him, but there was no response. Fear gripped his little heart as he huddled under a bush, feeling more alone than ever.

Just when Woolly thought all hope was lost, he heard a familiar voice calling his name. It was the shepherd! Woolly's heart leaped with joy as he saw the shepherd coming toward him, his face full of concern and love. The shepherd had left the other ninety-nine sheep to find him, and he had searched high and low until he did.

With gentle hands, the shepherd scooped Woolly up and cradled him close. Woolly felt safe again, his fear melting away as the shepherd whispered comforting words. The journey back to the flock was short, but Woolly felt like he was floating on air. He had been lost, but now he was found.

As they returned to the flock, the other sheep gathered around, welcoming Woolly back with soft bleats. The shepherd smiled and spoke of his joy in finding the lost lamb. Woolly knew he was loved, not just by the shepherd but by everyone in the flock. And as he drifted off to sleep that night, nestled close to the others, he felt a deep sense of peace. He had been lost, but now he was home, and nothing could ever change that.

And so, Woolly learned that no matter how far he might stray, the shepherd would always come to find him, just like God's love would always bring him back.

CHAPTER TWO:
THE BIRDS OF THE AIR

In a cozy nest high up in an old oak tree lived a little sparrow named Pip. Pip was a tiny bird, full of energy, but he had one big worry. Every morning, as the sun peeked over the horizon, Pip would wonder, "Will I find enough food today?" He fluttered nervously from branch to branch, searching for seeds and crumbs, his heart heavy with worry.

One bright morning, as Pip was anxiously searching for breakfast, he noticed something unusual. The other birds in the forest were not flitting about as they usually did. Instead, they sat calmly on the branches, chirping happily and enjoying the warmth of the sun. Pip couldn't understand why they weren't worried like he was.

Curious, Pip flew over to an older bird perched nearby. "Why aren't you out searching for food?" Pip asked. "Aren't you afraid there won't be enough to eat?"

The older bird smiled kindly at Pip. "Why should I worry?" he said. "Look at the world around you. Do you see how the flowers bloom in the fields and the trees grow tall and strong? God takes care of them, just as He takes care of us. If He provides for the flowers and the trees, how much more will He care for you and me?"

Pip thought about the older bird's words as he looked around the forest. He saw the flowers swaying in the breeze, the trees standing tall and full of life, and the other birds peacefully enjoying their day. For the first time, Pip noticed how the world was full of God's provision, and how every creature had what it needed.

That day, Pip decided to trust in God's care. He still flew around the forest, searching for food, but now he did it with a heart full of faith instead of fear. Whenever he found a seed or a crumb, he gave thanks, knowing it was a gift from God. And whenever he felt worry creeping in, he remembered the words of the older bird and the peaceful forest around him.

As the days went by, Pip's worries faded. He learned that God always provided what he needed, just as He did for all His creatures. And with that trust in his heart, Pip found a new joy in each day, soaring through the skies without a care, knowing that he was always in the Creator's loving hands.

CHAPTER THREE:
THE WISE AND FOOLISH BUILDERS

In a peaceful forest clearing, two families of animals decided to build their new homes. The first family, the Rabbits, were known for their careful planning and thoughtful decisions. They searched high and low for the perfect spot and finally found a sturdy rock at the edge of the clearing. "This is the perfect place," said Father Rabbit. "Our home will stand strong here, no matter what happens."

The second family, the Squirrels, were excited to build their home quickly so they could start enjoying the sunny days ahead. They found a soft, sandy spot in the middle of the clearing and decided to build there. "This will be easy

to dig into," said Mother Squirrel. "We'll have our home
ready in no time!"

As the days went by, both families finished their homes.
The Rabbits' house on the rock was strong and secure,
with walls that were firmly set in place. The Squirrels'
house on the sand was cozy and comfortable, but the
foundation was not as firm.

One night, a big storm rolled into the forest. The wind
howled, the rain poured down, and the trees swayed in the
fierce wind. The Rabbits huddled together inside their
home, feeling safe and secure. The rock beneath them
didn't move, and their house stood firm against the storm.

But over in the Squirrels' home, things were different. As the rain soaked the sand, the ground beneath their house began to shift. The walls trembled, and soon, the entire house started to lean. With a loud crash, the house collapsed, and the Squirrels had to scurry out into the storm, looking for shelter.

When the storm finally passed, the Squirrels were wet and cold, but they were grateful to be safe. They looked at their home, now just a pile of wood and leaves, and realized that they had made a mistake. They had built on sand, which couldn't hold up against the storm.

The next day, the Squirrels decided to rebuild their home, but this time, they chose a new spot—right next to the Rabbits' house on the rock. With the Rabbits' help, they built a new home with a strong foundation that would stand firm no matter what storms might come.

From that day on, the Squirrels learned the importance of making wise choices. They understood that it's not just about how quickly you build but where you build that truly matters. And as they settled into their new home, they were thankful for the lesson they had learned about building on a solid foundation, just like building one's life on the strong foundation of faith.

CHAPTER FOUR: THE MUSTARD SEED

In a quiet corner of a vast field, a tiny mustard seed lay nestled in the soil. The seed was so small that it felt almost insignificant compared to the other seeds around it. "What can I ever become?" the seed wondered. "I'm just a tiny speck in this great big world."

But as the days passed, something amazing began to happen. The seed felt a warmth from the sun and a refreshing coolness from the rain. Slowly, it started to grow, first sending out tiny roots to drink from the earth, and then sprouting a small green shoot that reached toward the sky.

Day by day, the mustard seed grew taller and stronger. It pushed through the soil, stretching toward the sunlight, and soon it was no longer a tiny seed but a small plant. The other plants in the field noticed the mustard seed's growth and were amazed at how quickly it grew. But the mustard seed knew that it wasn't growing on its own—it was God who was helping it grow.

As the seasons changed, the small plant continued to grow until it became a large tree, its branches spreading wide and strong. Birds from all around the field came to rest in its branches, building nests and singing songs of praise. The mustard seed, now a mighty tree, looked back on its journey with wonder. "Who would have thought that I, the tiniest of seeds, could become such a great tree?"

The mustard tree realized that its size and strength were not because of anything it had done on its own, but because of the power of God. The seed had trusted in God's plan, and in doing so, it had grown into something much greater than it ever imagined.

As the birds chirped happily in its branches, the mustard tree knew that it had a special purpose—to provide shelter and rest for others. And it understood that just like the seed, every creature has the potential to grow into something wonderful when they trust in God's care.

This chapter teaches that no matter how small we might feel, with faith and trust in God, we can grow into something great. Just like the mustard seed, we all have potential within us that, with God's help, can become something beautiful and strong, providing support and

shelter to those around us.

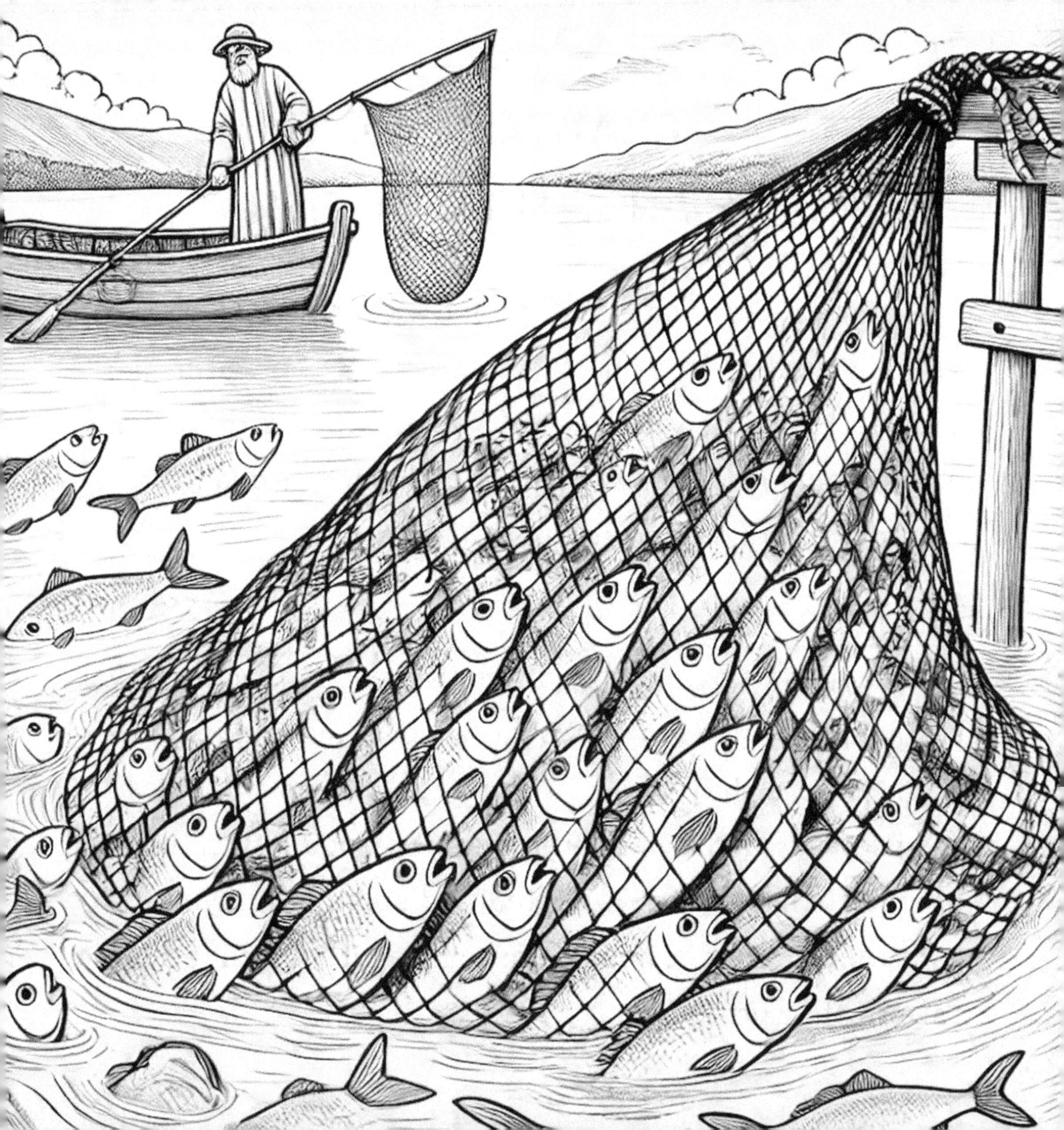

CHAPTER FIVE:
THE NET FULL OF FISH

In the deep, blue waters of a vast lake, a school of fish swam together, enjoying the coolness of the water and the beauty of their underwater world. Among them was a little fish named Finny, who loved to dart through the water, exploring every corner of the lake.

One day, as Finny and the other fish swam near the surface, they noticed a strange shadow moving above them. Before they could swim away, they found themselves caught in a large net that suddenly closed around them. The fish wriggled and squirmed, trying to escape, but the net held them tight as it was pulled up toward the surface.

Finny was frightened. He had never been caught in a net before, and he didn't know what was going to happen next. As the net was lifted out of the water, Finny and the other fish could see the fisherman waiting on his boat, ready to sort the catch.

The fisherman carefully untangled the fish from the net, placing some into one basket and letting others go back into the lake. Finny watched as the fisherman chose which fish to keep and which to release. He wondered why some were chosen and others were set free.

When it was Finny's turn, he was gently placed back into the water. As he swam away, he thought about what had just happened. The experience made him realize the importance of living a life that is pleasing to God, just as the good fish were chosen by the fisherman.

Finny shared his thoughts with the other fish when he returned to the school. "We should all strive to be like the good fish," he said, "so that when our time comes, we will be chosen too."

The fish understood Finny's message and agreed that the choices they made in their lives mattered. They decided to live each day in a way that would be pleasing to God, knowing that their actions had eternal significance.

As Finny swam through the lake, he felt a deep sense of peace. He knew that by living a life that honored God, he was making the right choices. And with that, Finny and his friends continued to swim in the deep, blue waters, thankful for the lesson they had learned about the importance of living a life that is pleasing to God.

This chapter teaches that our choices matter and that living a life that pleases God is the most important decision we can make. Just like the fish in the net, we are reminded that our actions have eternal significance, and by choosing to live according to God's will, we can be confident in His care and guidance.